The purpose of a mood board is to visually capture and communicate a specific mood, theme, or concept. It serves as a creative tool while planning the wedding of your dreams.

How to use *Captivating Bride* to find the wedding dress of your Dreams:

Think about how you want to display your mood board, then gather the supplies below.

- This book
- Corkboard, posterboard, blank wall (whatever you choose is fine)
- Glue, tape, pins - decide how you wish to attach items. Should they be permanent or will you want to move them around?
- Scissors
- Embellishments - ribbon, swatches of fabric, stickers, dried flowers or whatever else you can think of.

Now for the fun part! Create your vision. Use the photos in this book and the embellishments you have collected to create a collage that will help you visualize your dream dress.

Dive in, and see your dream wedding manifest!

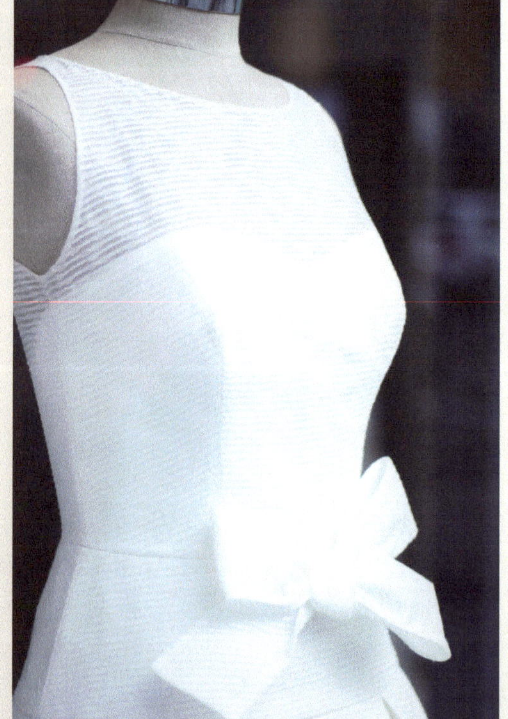

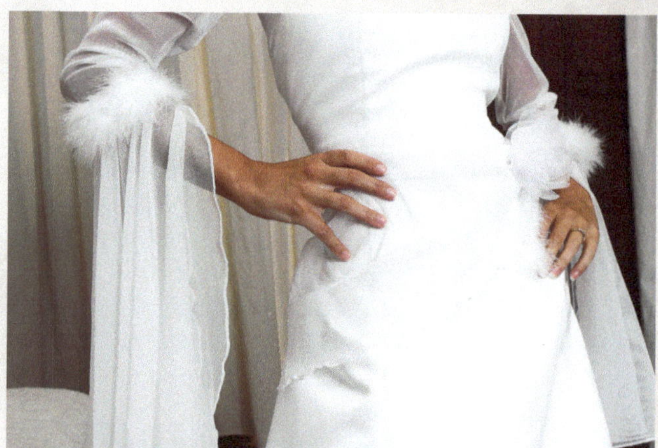

CARLOS PEREZ AI